HARALD MANTE

PHOTO DESIGN

PICTURE COMPOSITION IN BLACK-AND-WHITE PHOTOGRAPHY

VNR VAN NOSTRAND REINHOLD COMPANY
NEW YORK   CINCINNATI   TORONTO   LONDON   MELBOURNE

This book was originally published
in Germany under the title "Bildaufbau"
by Otto Maier Verlag, Ravensburg, 1970
Translation by E. F. Linssen SZS FRES FRPS
Copyright © 1971 by Focal Press Limited
Library of Congress Catalog Card Number 70-136113
ISBN 0-442-25150-5
Printed and bound in Spain
Published by Van Nostrand Reinhold Company
a division of Litton Educational Publishing, Inc.
450 West 33rd Street, New York, NY 10001
Van Nostrand Reinhold Limited
1410 Birchmount Road, Scarborough,
Ontario MIP 2E7, Canada

16 15 14 13 12 11 10 9 8 7 6 5 4 3 2

Printer industria gráfica sa
Tuset, 19   Barcelona
Sant Vicenç dels Horts 1977
Depósito legal B. 32204-1977
Printed in Spain

Contents

7 Preface
9 About this book

I. Format
10 Looking at pictures: size and distance
12 Viewing an area: eye movements
14 Viewing an area: optical illusions
16 Viewing an area: the general impression
18 Picture shape: square
20 Picture shape: rect-angular
22 Choice of shape: horizontal or vertical
24 Picture shape: narrow

II. Spot
26 The spot
28 The shape of the spot
30 Disturbing spots
32 The double spot
34 Visual line
36 Visual triangles
38 Visual triangles (variants)
40 The spot: visual shapes

III. Line
42 How a line is produced
44 Lines: basic types
46 Horizontal lines
48 Heavy horizontal lines
50 Vertical lines
52 Rising diagonal lines
54 Falling and intersect-ing diagonals

56 Oblique lines
58 Types of line
60 Irregular lines, varying thickness
62 Contrasting lines
64 Line groupings
66 Lines and visual shapes
68 Lines and visual shapes (variants)

IV. Shapes
70 Triangle
72 Circle
74 Square
76 Rectangle
78 Irregular shapes
80 Contrasting shapes
82 Detail
84 Extrapolation of partial shapes

V. Contrast
86 Spot and line
88 Spot, line and shape
90 Medial section: spatial distribution
92 Medial section: dis-tribution of numbers
94 Contrasting sizes and numbers
96 The horizon
98 Foreground and back-ground unsharpness
100 Blur due to movement
102 Wide angle lenses
109 Telephoto lenses

106 Technical data

In order to teach the fundamentals of any art form one needs to return to the elements in their abstract form, analyse them and then a synthesis can evolve. One searches to learn photography as in the other arts but no art can stand through the technique alone. The design and concept of placement, arrangement order of the line, the space, the depth and other factors are the elements to which we are striving for a creative picture. Here in Harald Mante's book "Bildaufbau — Gestaltung in der Fotografie" we submit to his careful analysis of the elements of an image and we see excellent photographic examples created in their simplicity to give you, the reader, a better understanding of photography. It is not enough for him just to show the images here; he carefully displays in a graphic manner the elements within the two dimensional plane that creates the photographic image. I have often found it necessary in teaching to have such a book in order for the student to realize his personal work through a design concept and not merely the "copying the master" concept. Here in its simplicity and lucid explanations and illustrations "Bildaufbau" achieves the purpose of its author, Harald Mante.

Alan Porter
Editor CAMERA magazine
Lucerne/Switzerland

Every branch of art—be it painting or sculpture, drama, music or whatever—is subject to the same fundamental, and therefore unchanging, laws of expression. Whether it is a spot which dominates an area, a figure on the stage, or a sound in the auditorium; whether a contrast is one of loud against soft, fast against slow, rough against smooth or large against small, the fundamental art principle remains the same. It is only the medium through which it is realized that varies from one discipline to another.

Thus, for instance, in Volume 2 of the Bauhaus book series—*Pädagoisches Skizzenbuch* by Paul Klee—and to an even greater extent in Volume 9—*Punkt und Linie zu Fläche* by Wassily Kandinsky—the artistic elements in two-dimensional creative composition are surveyed and analysed.

In the present book, the aim has been in some measure to apply these findings to photography. The compositional elements (format, point, line, surface, variation of contrast) are dealt with in so far as they affect the creation and criticism of a photograph. In order that this analysis might not be lost in tedious abstract generalities, it has been divided up into 48 individual sections, each section occupying a double spread, illustrated by a picture which is dominated by the particular compositional element to which the section is devoted.

It is, however, only rarely that any individual compositional feature is outstandingly dominant in any one picture: the impact is usually due to a number of different features. In the row of diagrams that appear beneath each picture, therefore, other compositional elements are shown which contribute points of emphasis to the composition, in addition to that forming the subject of the page.

These specific elements should not, however, be construed in too literal and narrow a sense. If, for example, a vertical is mentioned, this must not be taken to infer a continuous straight line from top to bottom of the picture! A standing figure, or some upright object, is sufficient to give the impression of a vertical line, and the same holds good for other compositional features.

The simpler the subject of a photograph and the compositional features utilized, the more important even the most minute details become. Nevertheless, the compositional devices described must not be looked upon as formulae for instant success: even strictly followed, they can never be an automatic means to artistic production. At most they may assist in imparting to the work a rhythmic and logical construction.

It is up to the individual to use his talent and perception as well as these basic rules, to create photographs of outstanding power of expression and communication, and so attain artistic success.

Wiesbaden, March 1969
Harald Mante

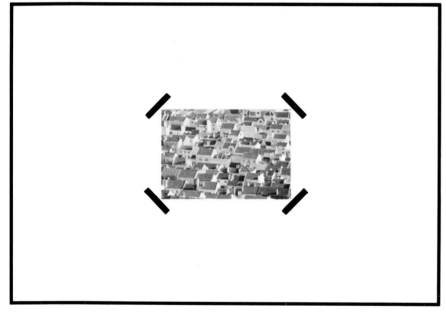

In looking at a picture, the viewing distance from the eyes should be twice the length of the diagonal of the picture. Since the normal reading distance is from 12 to 16 inches, the ideal size for a photograph or printed reproduction would be from 3½ × 4¾ in. (diagonal about 6 in.) to 4½ × 6¼ in. (diagonal 8 in.). When illustrating brochures, magazines, books, etc., these dimensions are important.

Pictures which are too small become mere spots: if too large—as, for example, a double spread in a picture book or illustrated magazine—they are for the most part examined only in detail, because it may become impracticable to view them at the requisite distance.

The full page illustrations of this book should be viewed from about 20 inches, that is, at arm's length. At any shorter distance it is not possible to take in the whole area of the picture without "scanning" it.

When a picture is too small, as for example the contact print shown above, or when a larger picture is viewed at too great a range in relation to its format, perception goes beyond the picture limits, taking in only a meaningless pattern of light and dark areas.

If the subject presented is clear and readily intelligible, the 3½ × 4¾ in. format will suffice. But where it comprises a large number of individual features enlargement must be more generous: its upper limit usually depends on technical considerations and the nature of the subject.

Visual shapes 40

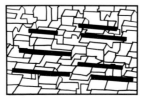

Verticals 50

Oblique lines 56

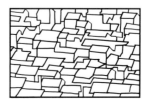

Detail 82

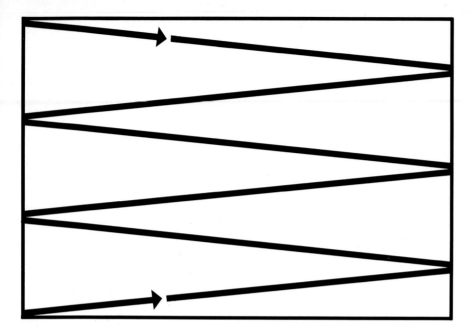

The two diagrams above illustrate the movements of the eyes when first viewing a rectangle or a square: *Upper*, scanning the area from left to right and *Lower*, diagonally. As with reading, the eyes commence their journey across the picture area in the left-hand top corner. This "reading routine" is fostered if there is a bright area at the left-hand side of the picture (or best of all, in the top left-hand corner). However, this area should not be too isolated: it is better if the eye is led into the picture by a succession of other bright features. Such constraint upon the eye to follow a path of light tones is well illustrated in the accompanying picture across a field: here it is simple and dominant, and acts in a counter direction to the normal "reading" scanning of the eye.

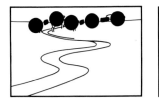

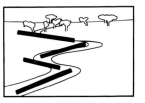

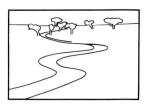

Visual line 34   Horizontals 46   Verticals 50   Oblique lines 56   Horizon 96

The movements of the eyes in scanning an area are, unconsciously, always the same. Nevertheless, where the composition possesses a dominant line pattern, as in the two pictures here, an optical illusion may occur.

In the picture on page 15, the lines of paving, and on this page the black trunk of the tree at the bottom of the picture gives the impression of having come into the picture from below. Wide angle lenses (see page 102) accentuate this effect by emphasising the foreground and diminishing the scale of background. Only after the first startling effect has died away does the eye begin to concentrate on other details in the image.

Diagonals 52

Oblique lines 56

Visual line 34

Horizontals 46

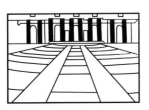

Verticals 50

Oblique lines 56

Triangle 70

Detail 82

When the eye is prevented by dark areas on the left, left and top, on three sides (as in the landscape), or on all four sides (as in the old town alley picture) from normal entry into the picture area, a surprising and odd effect is produced. It is possible in this way to lend a subject a more striking effect or even to obtain a picture which no longer corresponds with reality. The dark frame around the old town subject strengthens our impression of what a narrow alley is like. In the landscape, the darkness at the edge of the field, as also the light radiating from the centre outwards, creates a somewhat unreal atmosphere. Depending upon the subject, this impression can even approach the uncanny.

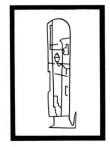
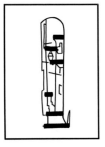
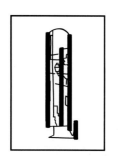
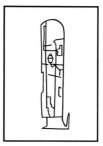

Darkness   Horizontals 46   Verticals 50

Darkness

Horizontals 46

Circular arc 72

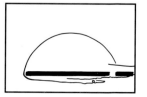
Horizon 96

Picture shape: square

There are two "normal" picture shapes: the variable rectangle and the invariable square. The square is the format of absolute symmetry. The all too well-balanced 1:1 side relationship calls for a very rigorous allocation of space.

The square format compositions of the Romanesque and the Baroque style in art show completely uniform distribution within the area, the one, however, being static, and the other dynamic in character. Any serious irregularity in the distribution of points, lines, and masses within the square will shift the centre of gravity in such a way that it may more or less destroy the character of the square. As only a few subjects are really appropriate to this format, composing a square picture is not easy. In practice, negatives taken with square format cameras are often subsequently enlarged to a (horizontal or vertic-al) rectangular format, or square prints are trimmed to rectangular shapes by book and magazine editors when they are reproduced. If a photographer is accustomed to composing his picture when shooting so as to fill the frame, in most cases any later trim will spoil the composition. The only advantage of the square format is that it relieves the photographer of the need to choose the ultimate format when actually taking the photograph, and indeed he must, in so far as he wishes to make commercial use of his pictures, always reckon with the probability that his square pictures will be trimmed.

Our example of the four rows of four bottles is ideal for the square format. The uniform distribution of the bottles over the area permits the eye to travel freely along horizontal, vertical and diagonal paths. The actual appeal of the picture, however, lies in the irregular distribution of the straws. This irregularity is needed to make an interesting play of points and lines on what would otherwise be a monotonous pattern, while remaining sufficiently restrained not to spoil the character of the square.

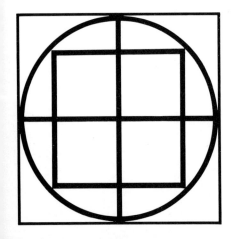

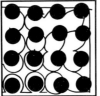 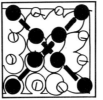  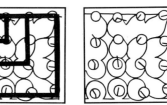 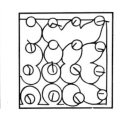

Visual lines 34   Diagonals 52   Oblique lines 56   Squares 74

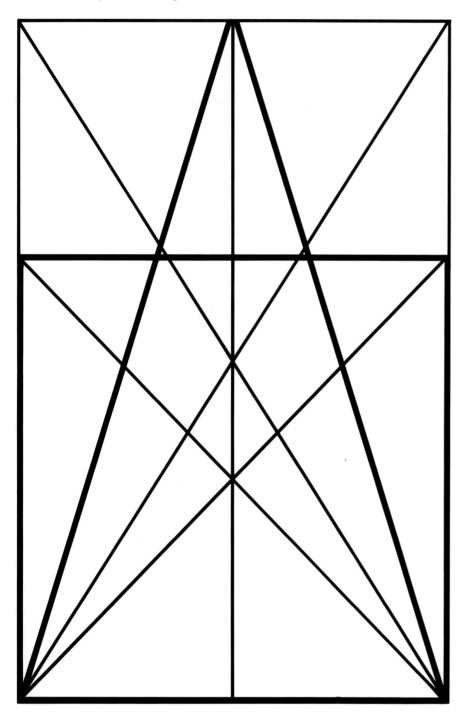

With its infinitely variable side relationship, the rectangle is the most universal and therefore the most favoured shape for pictorial composition. The Gothic style of composition employs a vertical rectangle with special emphasis on squares, triangles and diagonals.

The composition is bound up with the visual impression. The lines do not have to be visible throughout their length, for the eye and the imagination fill in any missing portions. Indications are all that is necessary, as can be seen in the picture on page 21. Here the counter diagonal from upper left to lower right is indicated by the tree and the fold in the cloth.

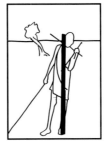

Vertical 50   Diagonals 52   Triangle 70   Square 74

The rectangle, offering as it does the choice of a horizontal or a vertical picture, provides the best medium for making the format suit the subject, thereby supporting and developing the photographic conception. These two examples illustrate how differently the same subject can be presented, and how varied the effect conveyed by choosing a vertical or horizontal shape. The horizontal format suggests tranquillity, depth, and cold: the vertical format action, proximity, warmth. In this connection, read also the discussion of horizontals and verticals on pages 46 to 50, the influence of which, one way or the other, applies equally to the rectangle.

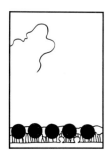

Visual line 34

Horizontals 46

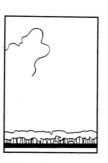

Verticals 50

Horizon 96

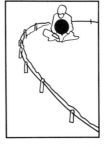
Dominating spot 26

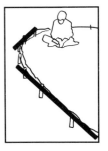
Verticals 50

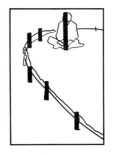
Oblique lines 56

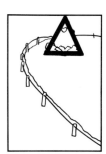
Triangle 70

Picture shape: narrow

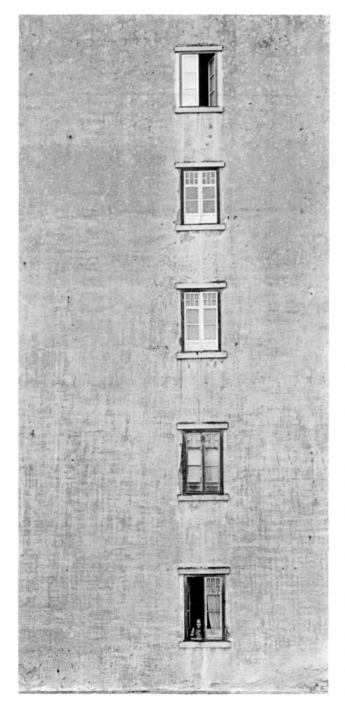

With certain subjects the rectangle lends itself to emphasis of the pictorial message (the vertical represents activity; the horizontal, quietude), and even extremely narrow formats are acceptable.

Thus, in the picture of the tenement the very narrow format accentuates the impression of height and confinement.

In contrast, the narrow horizontal format opposite enhances the atmosphere of relaxation and peacefulness in the park.

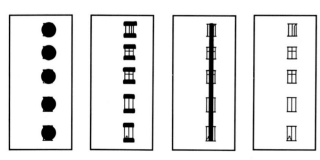

Visual line 34   Horizontals 46   Verticals 50

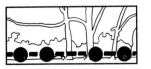

Visual line 34

Horizontals 46

Verticals 50

Oblique lines 56

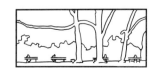

The spot

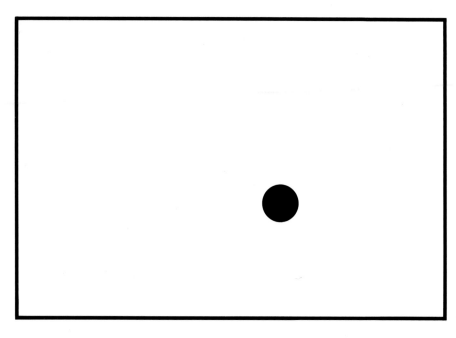

"The spot is the outcome of the first contact of the tool with the material, with the basic surface". (Wassily Kandinsky).

In photography, light takes over the role of the tool.

The spot ".... firmly maintains its position and shows not the slightest inclination to move in any direction, either horizontal or vertical." (Kandinsky).

Nevertheless, its position within the picture space is very important. One single spot on a neutral area immediately dominates it. This instantly claims attention, and the eye scans the picture area to establish its position in relation to the edges and corners of the picture.

When the subject itself exhibits strong contrasts, as in the picture on page 27 where the large dark area of the background contrasts with the small bright subject, it is an advantage to place the spot in the medial section. The harmonic position of the spot then supports the effect of spatial contrast. If a spot is placed too centrally in the picture space it may become an axis around which the picture appears to rotate. If, on the other hand, it is too close to the edge, it can upset the general balance.

The point at which a spot becomes a mass depends upon its size in relation to the picture area and any other masses in the composition. When contrasted with very fine lines, as in the case of the dark doorway and the delicate balcony railings in the picture on the left, the spot becomes a mass.

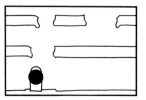

Dominating spot

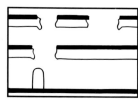

Horizontals 46

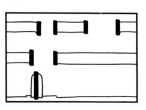

Verticals 50

Dominating spot

Horizontals 46

Verticals 50

Oblique lines 56

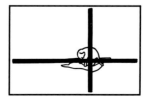

Medial section 90

Contrasting sizes 94

The shape of the spot

Grouping of spots

Oblique lines 56

Line and shape 66

A spot does not have to be round. It can assume a variety of shapes.

"The realm of the spot is unbounded" (Kandinsky). Besides the circular shape, other geometrical figures occur in composition, such as the triangle, the square, the rectangle, and so forth; or irregular shapes may develop. The outline of the spot too may be irregular and jagged, and the jags themselves may be variously related in size.

The two examples on page 28 illustrate spot groupings wherein—especially in the case of the suckling piglets— a new, and larger spot is formed which has an irregular outline.

The boat on page 29 is central in the picture space, and this emphasizes the calmness and tranquillity of the scene. The horizontal stabilizing effect of the boat reduces the tendency of the picture to turn about a central point.

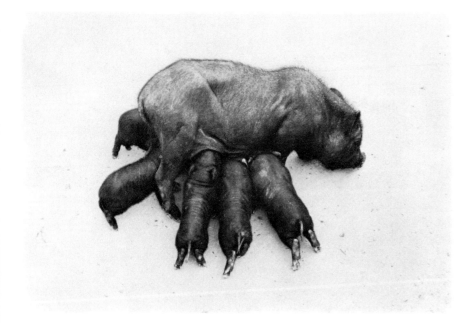

Grouping of spots

Horizontals 46

Oblique lines 56

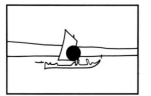
Central spot

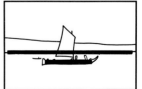
Horizontals 46

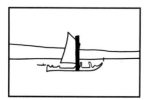
Verticals 50

Oblique lines 56

Triangle 70

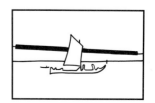
Horizon 96

Disturbing spots

It is possible for even a visually animated area to be dominated by a single spot. This would happen with the head of the child in the picture on this page were it not for the bright spot created by the scrap of paper in the left-hand bottom corner which catches the eye and thereupon becomes the dominating feature of the picture.

Disturbing spots of this kind immediately attract the eye (a typical instance of this is dust on an enlargement).

Light spots can be removed by retouching. With dark spots it is more difficult, unless the spot is on a plain white background and can be taken out with reducer.

In the case of the picture on page 31 the only way to eliminate the offending spot was to trim it off.

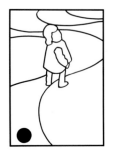

Disturbing spot

Spot 26

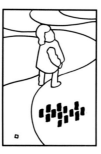

Curving line 58

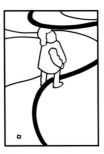

Detail 82

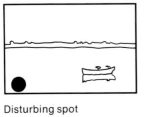

Disturbing spot

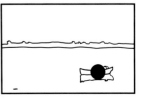

Dominating spot 26

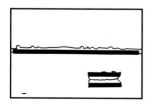

Horizontals 46

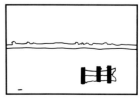

Verticals 50

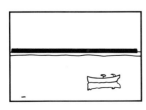

Horizon 96

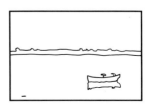

The double spot

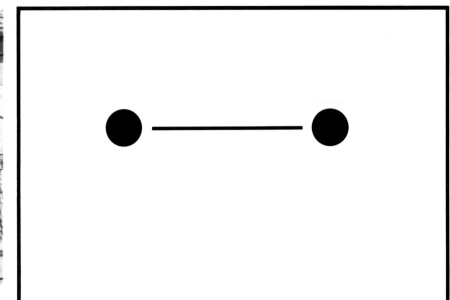

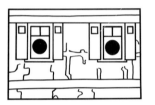

Double spot

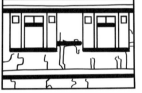

Horizontals 46

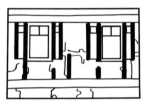

Verticals 50

Whenever two spots occur in the same picture the eye becomes restless and wanders from one to the other.

Thus in the normal portrait, for example, it is very difficult to achieve a picture of artistic merit, as distinct from a mere record. It is true that we have become accustomed to the presence in every face of two spots of equal importance—the two eyes. Nevertheless, in a badly executed portrait they can be most obtrusive. In a double portrait, (two heads = two spots) composition is far from easy. Only visible action or an obvious relationship between the two persons photographed, with perhaps also the inclusion of foreground or background in the composition, can provide the conditions essential to an artistically satisfactory result.

Visual line 34

Horizontals 46

Oblique lines 56

Triangles 70

Irregular shapes 78

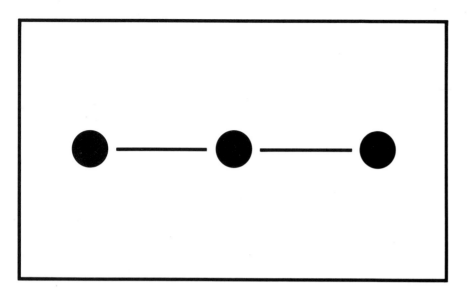

If, in a picture, at least three spots occur in a row the eye will construct an imaginary line through them. The spots need not be the same size, shape, or distance apart. Even considerable distances between spots, and from the spots to the edge of the picture can be bridged by visual lines.

These visual lines may be straight, as in the photograph on page 35, or they may be curved. The eye follows the line of the spots so compulsively that the visual line can even change its direction. In the picture on this page the course of the chain of spots runs first from left to right, changing direction half way to rise from right to left.

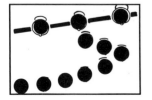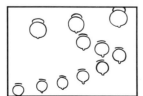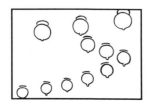

Visual line, curved

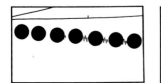

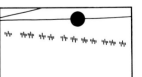

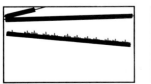

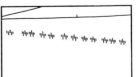

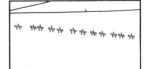

Visual line   Disturbing spot 30   Oblique lines 56

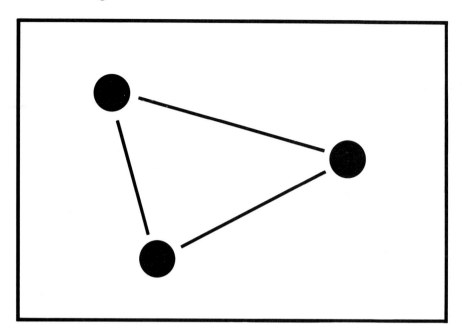

A suitable arrangement of at least three spots creates a visual triangle in the mind. Here again, the shape and size of the spots may differ somewhat without altering the effect. An important factor, however, is the position of the triangle within the picture area. To achieve a satisfying and balanced effect none of the sides of the triangle should be parallel to any side of the picture. Provided this is the case, none of the three corners of the triangle achieves any serious directional significance.

Such a visual triangle necessarily creates further visual areas, between the triangle and the edges of the picture, again mostly triangular.

In the case of subjects where movement of specific features, be they human figures, animals, or vehicles, causes continual change in the composition, it is always worthwhile waiting a little and taking several shots in succession. In the short series of the cows on the sea-shore about ten minutes elapsed between the first and third exposures. In the meantime the three cows on the right hand side formed into a closed group and the single cow had moved forward a little, thereby allowing the disturbing rock on the left to be trimmed off.

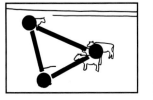

Visual triangle

Secondary visual triangles

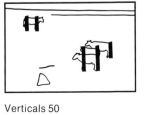

Horizontals 46

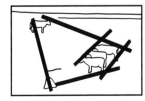

Verticals 50

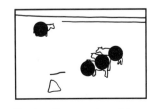

Oblique lines 56

Contrasting numbers 94

Visual triangles (variants)

This series is a good example of patience rewarded, and also of visual triangles with directional effect. In the course of half an hour over twenty photographs were taken. The most interesting configurations, from the first to the final successful shot are shown in the contact series at the bottom of this page.

In the visual triangles formed, in each case one of the sides runs parallel to the edge of the picture, thus strongly emphasizing the corners and giving the triangle a feeling of movement. In the examples on page 38 this movement is from left to right. On page 39 the downward-pointing triangle gives a strong suggestion of movement in that direction.

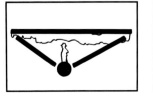

Visual triangle

Dominating spot 26

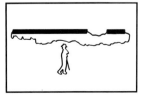

Horizontals 46

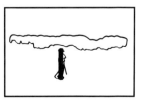

Verticals 50

Detail 82

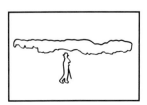

The spot: visual shapes

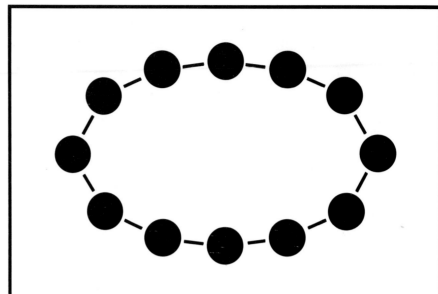

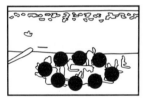

Visual shape

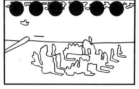

Visual line 34

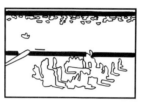

Horizontals 46

Any number of spots depending upon their distribution over the picture, can create for the viewer one or more visual shapes. As a rule, such shapes are the random and haphazard creation of the lines which the eye traces through the spots. In some cases however the distribution of these spots forms geometrical figures such as a circle, ellipse or square. The effect of such shapes depends upon their relative size within the picture shape. In the general view reproduced on this page, the ellipse formed by the fishermen has only secondary function in the composition; the oblique line at the left of the picture and the visual line formed by the boats on the horizon are if anything more important. Only when the visual ellipse is brought to a central position and the competing elements trimmed out (page 41) does it dominate the picture.

It can then be seen that where the figures congregate more closely other, smaller visual shapes appear.

Visual ellipse

Smaller visual shapes

Verticals 50

Oblique lines 56

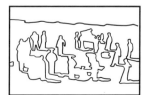

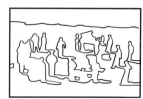

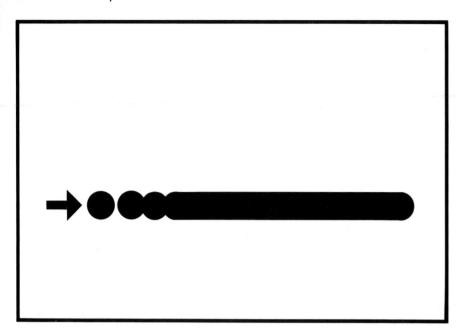

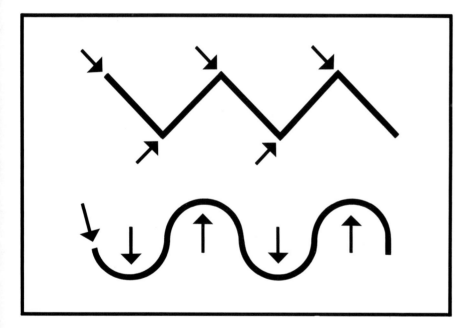

By the strictest definition, the line is the tracing of a point which is caused to move from its fixed position by one or more forces. From the static point is thus produced the dynamic line to which it exhibits the utmost conceivable contrast.

If only one force is active, the line will be straight. Any other kind of line is the effect of two, varying forces. A time exposure records a moving point of light as a line (page 43).

Thus, photography can show the creation of a line by a moving point.

Disturbing spot 30

Oblique lines 56

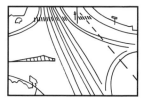

Line grouping 64

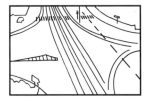

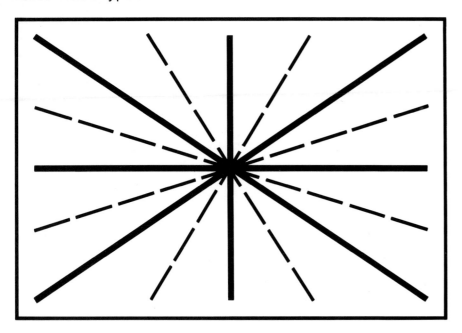

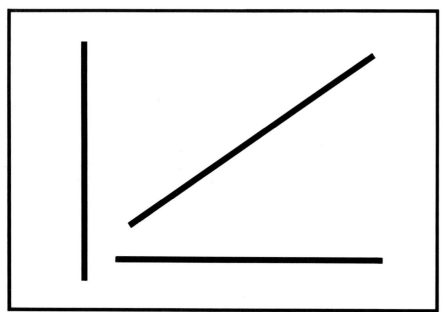

Straight lines may be divided into three main groups—horizontal, vertical, and diagonal. These three types are not alien to the picture format. Visually the horizontals and verticals are but the edges of the picture invading the picture space, while the diagonals merely follow the eye as it scans from corner to corner. Any straight line which does not fall into one of these categories is less integral with that format. Such oblique lines, and indeed, diagonals also, bring instability to the composition. This calls for the balancing effect of some horizontal or vertical elements.

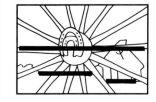

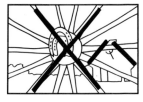

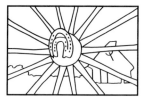

Basic types of line   Dominating spot 26   Horizontals 46   Oblique lines 56   Triangles 70

Horizontal lines

The simplest straight line is the horizontal. A single horizontal line in the picture space gives the impression of a natural horizon. A number of horizontals suggest distance and lead the eye successively into the most remote area.

The horizontal is a cool, restful, smooth line. It is most appropriate to a horizontal format which already possesses the same cool characteristic (page 47). Where a number of horizontal lines occur on a vertical format, a conflict arises between the cool lines and the warm format. The lines divide the picture space into a series of narrow horizontal areas thereby enhancing the visual impression of breadth (left).

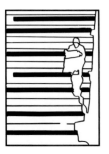
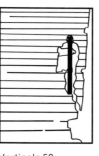

Horizontals   Dominating spot 26   Verticals 50   Oblique lines 56

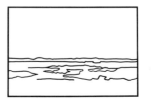

Horizontals   Verticals 50   Horizon 96

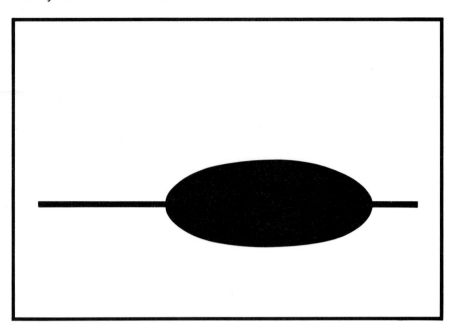

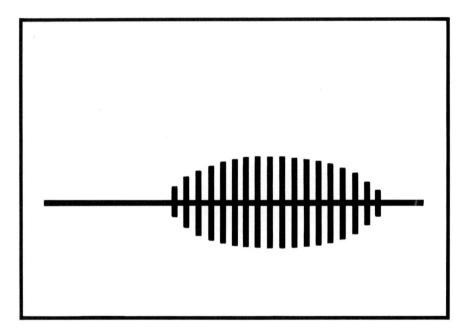

A broad horizontal line can, in certain circumstances, have a confining effect by demanding attention. A heavy dark streak has, for a person looking at it, something of the content of the vertical. It is reminiscent of a belt of forest land, or a fence consisting of a large number of closely spaced slats which, when seen from a distance coalesce into a horizontal dark band. In the photograph on page 49 it can be very clearly seen from the reflection in the water how the dark band is in fact made up of a great number of verticals.

The suggestion of spatial depth associated with the horizontal is somewhat offset by the influence of the verticals.

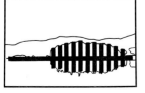
Verticals 50

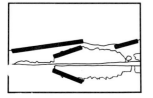
Oblique lines 56

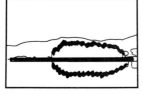
Contrasting lines 62

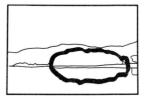
Irregular shape 78

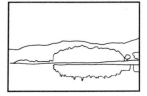

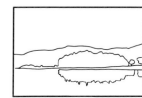

Vertical lines

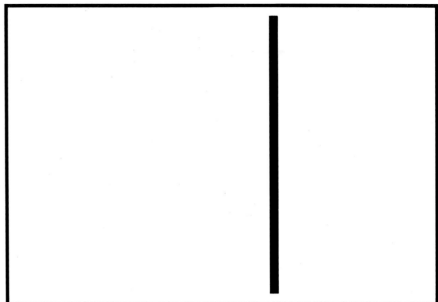

The effect and character of the horizontal "... is completely in contrast to that of the vertical at right angles to it, which replaces flatness by height, and so coolness by warmth." (Kandinsky) Verticals are completely lacking in any suggestion of distance. Every vertical line stands uncompromisingly before the eyes which are thereby inhibited from wandering into the distance, being brought up short, as it were, by a barrier.

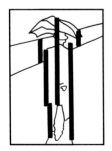

Verticals   Oblique lines 56

Verticals

Dominating spot 26

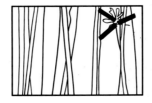

Oblique lines 56

Line groupings 64

Visual surfaces 66

Rising diagonal lines

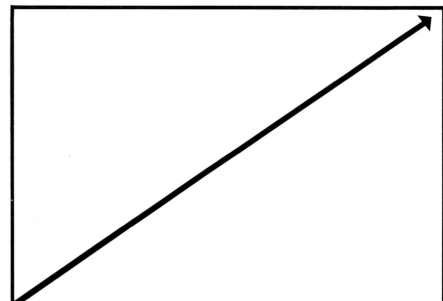

Rising diagonal lines

Verticals 50

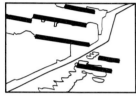

Oblique lines 56

In between the horizontals and the verticals lie the third group of straight lines—the diagonals. On the psychological temperature scale they come half way, a compromise between cool and warm.

The diagonal has a strongly stimulating effect, and in order that this may not lead the eye too rapidly out of the picture the restraint of a horizontal or vertical is needed.

The most harmonious to the eye is the rising diagonal from left bottom to right top. This is least in need of the horizontal-vertical restraint.

The accompanying pictures show two ways of treating the rising diagonal. Above the diagonal runs directly from the left-hand bottom corner to the right-hand top—strictly according to rule. Much more interesting however, is the case of the picture on page 53. Here, the diagonal is not from corner to corner, but begins part way up the left hand side and ends a little to the left of the right-hand top corner. This does not detract from the visual effect of rising from bottom left to top right. The curve in the shore line forms an irregular subsidiary line and even, to a degree, acts as a counter-diagonal.

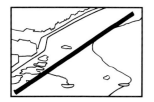

Diagonal

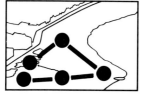

Visual shapes 40

Verticals 50

Oblique lines 56

Contrasting lines 62

Falling and intersecting diagonals

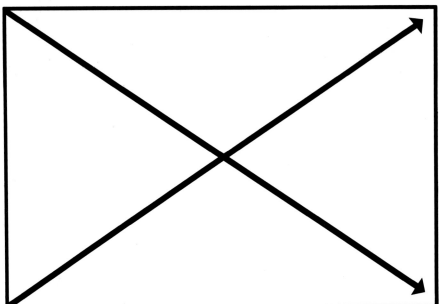

The falling diagonal from top left to bottom right has a specially compulsive effect. Here the horizontal-top left to bottom right has vertical constraint must definitely be exercised as otherwise the eye tends to travel right down the diagonal and out of the picture.

In the example on this page, apart from the visual horizontal, and the vertical figures of the fishermen, the really compulsive restraint comes from the counter-movement of the hurrying figures which offsets the effect of the falling diagonal.

The combination of diagonal and counter diagonal almost always arises in photographs of streets (page 55).

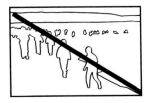

Falling diagonal   Horizontals 46   Verticals 50

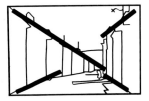

Diagonals

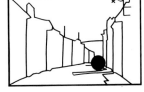

Dominating spot 26

Verticals 50

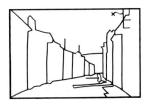

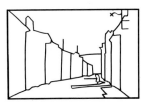

Oblique lines

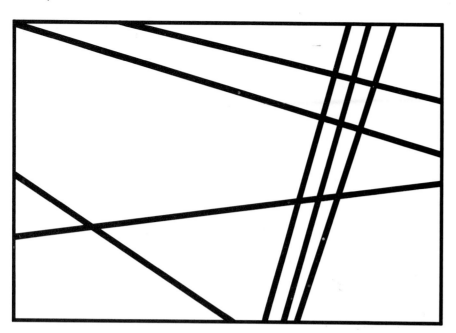

Straight lines at an oblique angle somewhere between the horizontal, vertical and diagonal are alien to the format. They are far removed in character from the restful spot which is part and parcel of the composition and bring great instability to the composition. This calls for the restful restraint of a horizontal or vertical line. In the picture on page 57 only the presence of a few verticals gives stability to the restless oblique lines. In the landscape on this page the oblique lines present less of a problem, because they converge from left and right on the centre. Here the stabilizing influence comes from the horizontals of the plain and the clouds.

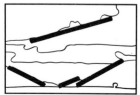

Oblique lines

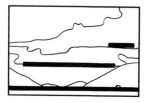

Dominating spot 26

Horizontals 46

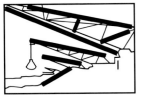
Oblique lines

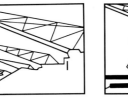
Dominating spot 26

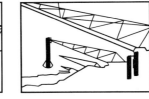
Horizontals 46

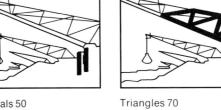
Verticals 50

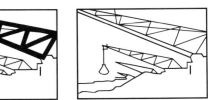
Triangles 70

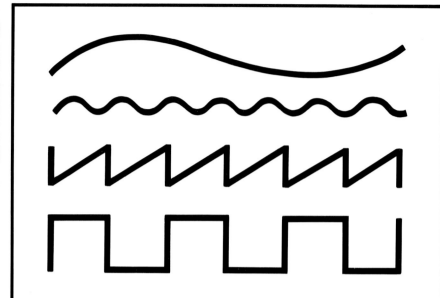

Hard lines

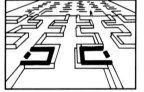
Visual shapes 66

Spot and lines 86

All straight lines, as we have seen, are the result of the action of a force on a point. Only if a second force comes into action can the line change its direction, and, depending upon the relative strengths and directions of the two forces, may assume the greatest variety of rhythmic shapes.

To mention but a few, these may take the form of small and large undulations, curves, zigzag and angular lines, and of course every kind of irregular line.

The line acquires an expression of its own, and every line, according to its character, creates a different impression on the viewer. The hard, angular lines of the photographs on this page, assisted by the play of light and shade, convey a harsher message than the relatively soft lines of the picture on page 59. Incidentally, this example illustrates particularly well a characteristic of lines which run from one edge of the picture to another which was not previously mentioned: the format becomes divided into sections.

Any line which runs from one edge to another divides the picture into two sections, or, should it cross other lines, into more than two.

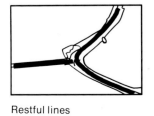

Restful lines

Oblique lines 56

Line grouping 64

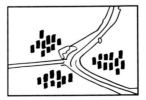

Detail 82

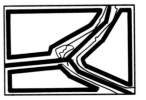

Lines and shapes 88

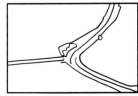

Irregular lines, varying thickness

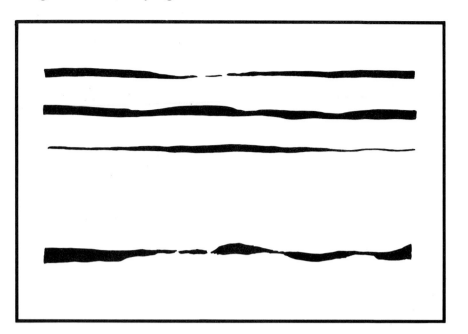

Irregular lines have the greatest individuality. This is particularly evident in a picture containing harsh black-and-white contrast (left). Here, however, as also in the picture on page 61, other artistic properties contribute in some way: the contrast of thick lines to thin, and (above all in the rock fissures on page 61) the variation in thickness of the lines, the swelling and shrinking almost to the point of completely disappearing.

A highly expressive line of this nature is also termed an artistic line.

Irregular lines

Visual shapes 66

Horizon 96

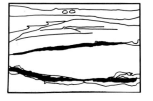

Lines of varying thickness

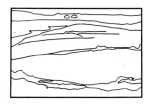

Horizontals 46

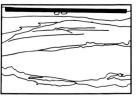

Oblique lines 56

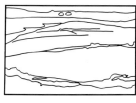

Horizon 96

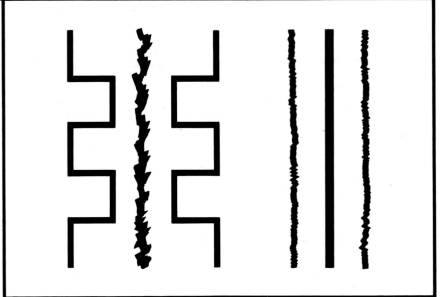

When lines of contrasting character are set one against their power of expression is heightened.

An angular line appears more so when placed in contrast with an irregular shaggy line, and vice versa.

In the picture on this page the tree appears still more bristly because it is close to the houses.

The example on page 63 shows the austere uprights of the masts transformed into zigzag lines by reflection in the water.

Contrasting lines

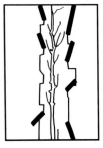

Verticals 50

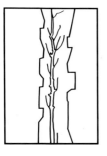

Oblique lines 56

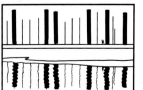

Contrasting lines

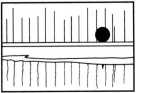

Dominating spot 26

Horizontals 46

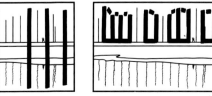

Verticals 50

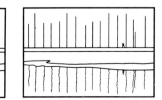

Visual shapes 66

Line groupings

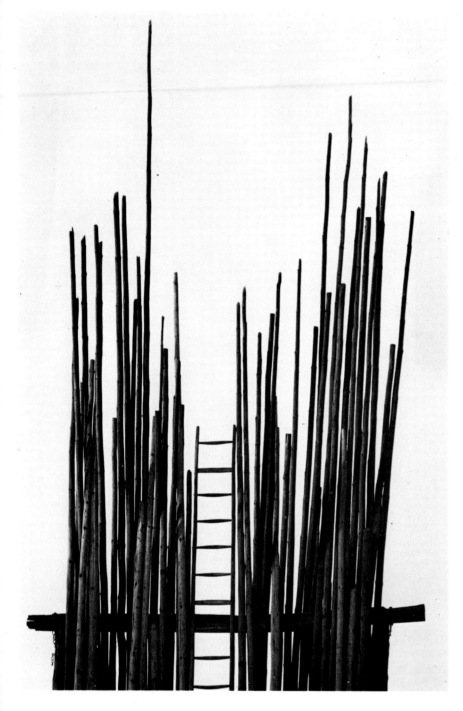

It often happens that a line is accompanied by a second, or several further lines. If these lines are close together the intervening spaces create a new set of (negative) lines. If they are well separated but parallel, they create visual shapes, which the eye completes by visually joining the ends together.

The photograph on this page shows the straight line accompanied by a family of strongly marked parallel lines. In this example both negative lines and visual shapes appear (see page 68), and the overall impression is static.

In the example on page 65, the accompanying line is the irregular trunk of the tree against the straight lines of the ladders. This irregular line, which crosses the straight lines, swings away from them, and in places runs parallel. The result, with the contrast in these lines is an overall dynamic effect.

Line groupings

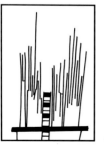

Horizontals 46

Verticals 50

Visual shapes 66

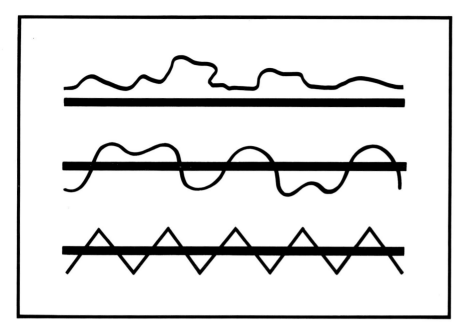

 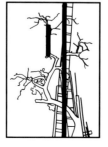  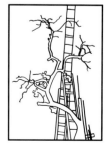

Irregular accompanying lines   Verticals 50   Visual shapes 66

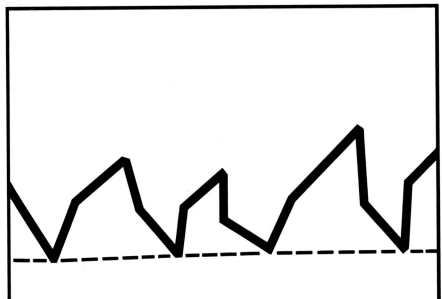

Visual shapes

Visual lines 34

Contrasting lines 62

An outstanding characteristic of the line, besides the division of space, is that it creates shape. Such a shape is complete when the line ultimately returns to its starting point. However it frequently happens that the line ends before reaching it, or changes course.

In this case, provided the two ends of the line are favourably placed, the eye steps in and supplies the missing section to complete the space.

In the case of the running flamingoes (above) the eye is greatly assisted by the favourably placed horizontal; with the help of this the line of the legs creates clear-cut triangular shapes.

In addition, the curved necks provide further visual shapes.

These visual shapes should not be too small in relation to the picture area. If they are, they cause instability in the composition. The ideal condition is where one large visual shape contrasts with other, smaller ones.

In the picture on page 67 the eye visualizes a large semi-circle joining the heads. Smaller visual shapes are formed by the spaces between the individual children and between the outstretched arms and legs.

Visual shapes

Visual line 34

Horizontals 46

Verticals 50

Lines and visual shapes (variants)

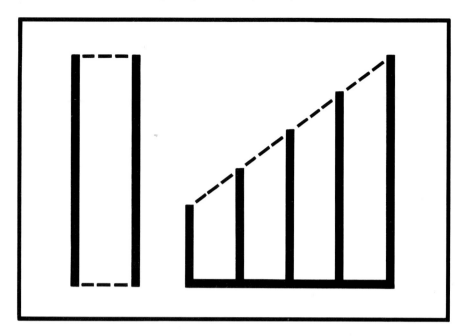

Visual shapes arise from any series of lines. In most cases the eye has only to supply one completing line, as in the example on page 69. In each case two vertical lines and one horizontal are already present. The shapes are completed by visually joining the tops of the telegraph poles.

Visual shapes can also be formed between adjacent lines or shapes. In the case of the riders (left) the eye visualizes the connecting lines at top and bottom.

Visual shapes

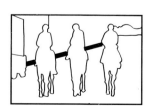

Verticals 50

Oblique lines 56

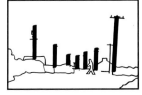

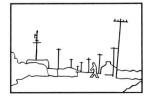

Visual shapes   Dominating spot 26   Horizontals 46   Verticals 50   Triangle 70

Shapes: the triangle

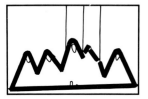
Triangles

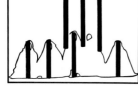
Verticals 50

Visual surfaces 56

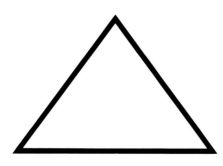

After the point and the line, the third element in composition is the shape. Here we must distinguish between the visual shape (pages 36 to 41 and 66 to 69) and the complete, solid shape. The solid shape may be made up of a single tone or several different tones.

The three basic shapes are the triangle, the circle and the square.

The triangle is an active shape. In its normal position (as a pyramid) the upward pointing apex suggests vertical movement. The directional significance of a triangle in the picture space has already been discussed under the visual triangle (page 36) and what was said there applies equally to the solid shape.

Where there is a series of triangles, as in the examples on this page and page 71, their visual counterparts, with their apices downward, have the opposite directional effect. In the case of the five women the black and the white triangles are equally striking, and the effects balance out.

On the other hand, the dark counter-triangles to the gables, especially as they are traversed by the chimneys, fail to offset the upward movement of the white gable.

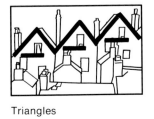
Triangles

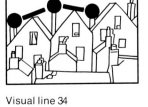
Visual line 34

Visual triangle 36

Verticals 50

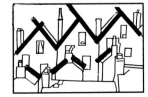
Oblique lines 56

Visual shapes 66

Shapes: the circle

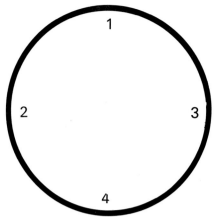

The circle is the symbol of eternity, without beginning or end. Of perfection and completeness.

Despite the fact that the circle has no beginning or end, nevertheless, for reasons of association, one does recognize in it certain fixed points: top and bottom (1 and 4 vertical), left and right (2 and 3, horizontal). From these come the semicircle and quadrant which, besides the full circle, often find application in typographic design, arts and crafts, architecture etc.

Where two circles abut, visual triangles are created. In the photograph on page 73, however, they are less apparent on account of the complicated background.

Circular shape

Horizontals 46

Verticals 50

Oblique lines 56

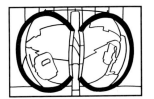

Circular shape

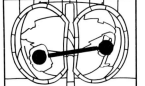

Two spots 32

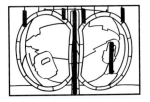

Verticals 50

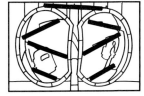

Oblique lines 56

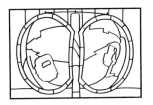

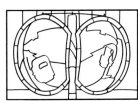

Shapes: the square

Although the square is not particularly suitable as a picture format (page 18), it does, nevertheless, often serve as a restful counterpoint in composition.

On page 75 the squares of the windows form a series of spots, creating a visual line. The risk of monotonous repetition is obviated by varying the tone values and internal arrangement.

Also, in the square partitioning of the window on (left) the individual squares are differentiated, in this case by the detail of their content.

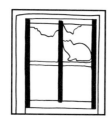

Squares   Horizontals 46   Verticals 50

Squares

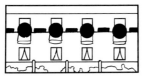

Visual line 34

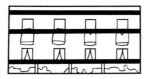

Horizontals 46

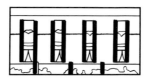

Verticals 50

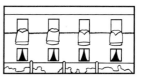

Triangles 70

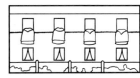

The variable rectangle is not only the most favoured shape for picture formats, it is also the most generally used of all geometrical figures. From paper formats and everyday articles to architecture and landscape planning, its applications far exceed those of the fundamental shapes—the triangle, circle and square. A rectangular feature within a rectangular picture space is a repetition of the format. In the photograph on page 77 the rectangle actually appears thirteen times in various sizes. The attraction of the picture lies in the alternate use of horizontal and vertical rectangles—the square window frame and the triangular shapes introduced by the curtains.

In the picture on the left the bare rectangular shape is disguised somewhat by the ornamental ironwork and the figure of the dog.

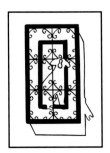
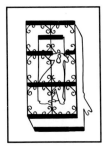
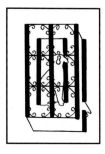
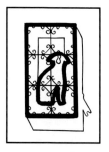

Rectangles   Horizontals 46   Verticals 50   Contrasting shapes 80

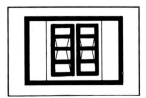

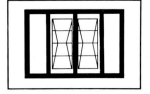

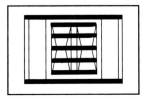

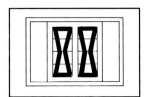

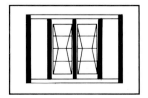

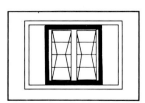

9 horizontal rectangles   4 vertical rectangles   Horizontals 46   Verticals 50   Triangles 70   Square 74

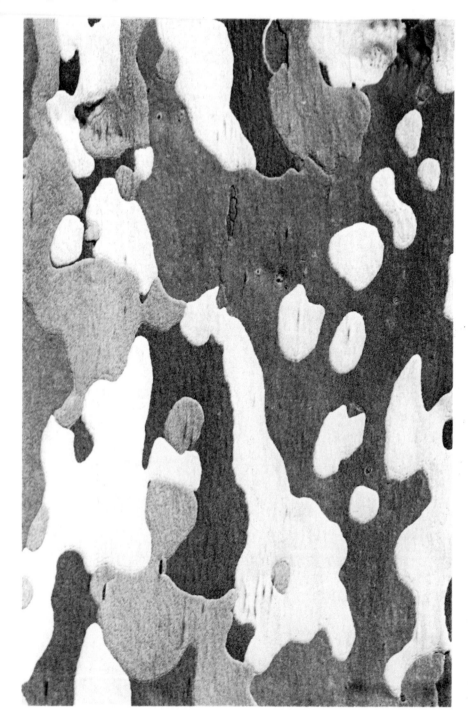

The "basic figures" and other geometrical shapes are the developments of civilization, while irregular shapes are mainly of natural origin. Almost all natural objects — men, animals, plants, landscapes, etc. — have completely irregular outlines.

The accompanying photographs of the bark of a tree and a coastal scene are examples of irregular shape formation.

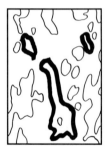
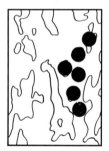

Irregular shapes   Visual line 34   Diagonals 52

Irregular shapes

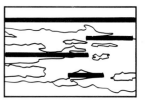

Horizontals 46

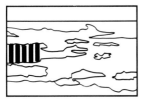

Verticals 48

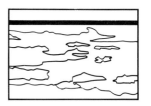

Horizon 96

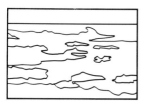

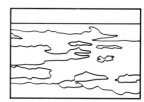

Shapes of differing character, as with lines (page 62) can be set off one against the other. The individual characteristics of shapes (e.g. triangle: activity, circle: restfulness, square: heaviness) are emphasized by contrast with one another but still more by contrast with an irregular shape.

Contrast already exists between the shape of the picture format and the content of most pictures. Moreover, this is not very noticeable except where the subject exhibits broad areas, e.g. a portrait on a neutral background (left).

In the photograph on page 81, against the quiet background of the wall the severe rectangular shapes of door and window stand out in contrast to the irregular shapes of the figures.

Contrasting shapes   Verticals 50   Oblique lines 56   Line groupings 64

Contrasting shapes

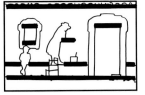

Horizontals 46

Verticals 50

Contrasting lines 62

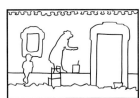

The effect of large areas in a picture does not depend only upon the shape of their outline, but also upon the nature of the detail within them.

Where such a large surface is seen in contrast with smaller shapes, lines or spots it may, without detriment, be quite uniform in tone. But should this contrast be lacking, or the picture consist only of this one area, there must be detail for a picture to result from a mere partition of the space. The thatched roof (bottom left) has a uniform detail structure in differing shades of grey without this involving any change of shape. In the crowd scene (page 83) which covers the whole picture space, the individual bright spots and concentrations of shadow create small visual shapes.

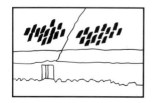

Detail within the space

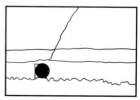

Dominating spot 26

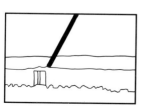

Oblique line 56

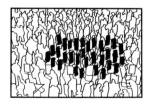

Detail within the space

Visual line 34

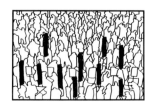

Verticals 50

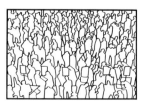

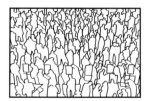

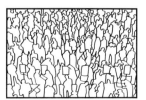

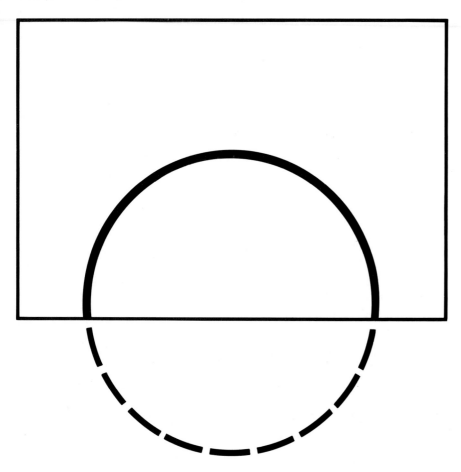

Normally a composition is complete within its format. Where the photograph includes a shape which can be continued in the viewer's imagination outside the picture area this represents the furthermost limit which can be achieved in pictorial composition.

In this process, imagination is often supported by our actual knowledge of the shape of the subject even though the picture shows only a part.

Often, shapes such as a triangle or a circle are partly cut off by the edge of the picture. These, too, are completed in the mind of the viewer.

Thus on page 33, the shape of the hat is completed in the imagination and the waggon wheel on page 85 is seen as a complete circle.

Extrapolation of shape

Verticals 50

Oblique lines 56

Triangles 70

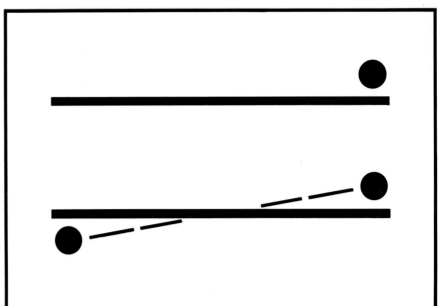

As can be seen from many of the preceding pictorial examples, the various forms of pictorial composition are not always employed in isolation, but far more often in combination.

If spots and lines occur simultaneously in a picture they compete for dominance. A spot at the foot of a perpendicular enhances its stability. If it is at the top, like the cat beside the little girl's head (left), the balance of the composition may be disturbed. The weight of the spot may appear to throw the vertical out of its true position.

Similarly, horizontal elements can be thrown out of balance by a spot at one end. If a second spot is placed opposite, at the other end, the horizontal will appear tilted.

The photograph on page 87 shows horizontals and oblique lines, spots and visual obliquity in a balanced composition.

Spot and line

Horizontals 46

Vertical 50

Triangle 70

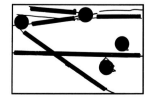
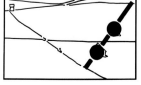
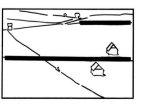
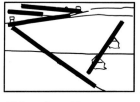
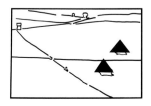
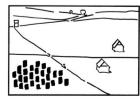

| Spot and line | Visual line 34 | Horizontals 46 | Oblique lines 56 | Triangles 70 | Detail 82 |

Spot, line and shape

Spot, line and shape

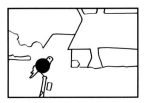

Dominating spot 26

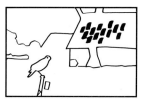

Detail 82

Strictly speaking, spots and lines never occur alone, because the picture space will already have been divided up into areas by one or more lines. Moreover, where there is a number of spots these may themselves form (visual) shapes. (See page 67).

In the landscape on page 89 spots occur in visual lines and shapes, as well as with actual lines and shapes. The upper photograph on this page shows spot set against surface, with only an indication of the line of the chair back. The contrast of spot and line is further emphasized by the contrast in sharpness and unsharpness. With the stone blocks in the lower picture, the individual shapes of the blocks are outlined by heavy shadow lines. In addition their surface is divided into countless small patterns by finer lines.

Lines and shapes

Rising diagonal 52

Oblique lines 56

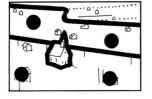 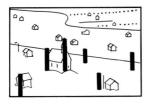 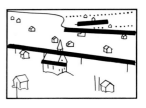  

Spot, line and shape   Visual shapes 40   Verticals 50   Oblique lines 56

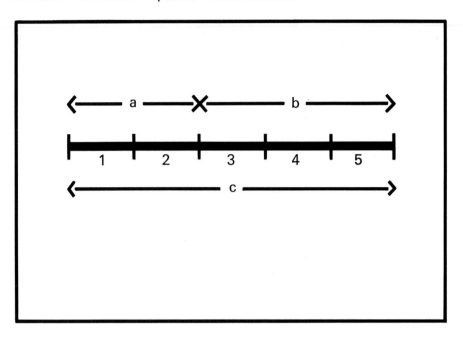

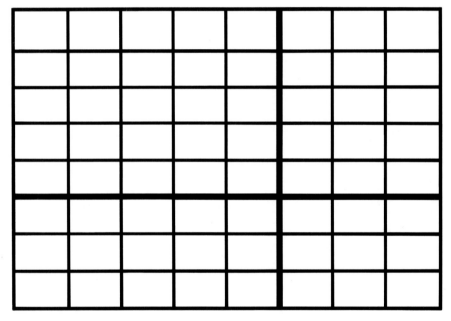

The division of a line by a medial section results in balanced dimensions. A line is divided so that the ratio of the smaller section to the larger is equal to that of the larger section to the whole line. Thus: $a:b = b:c$ (see this page, top).

For the purposes of pictorial composition it is most usual to employ an approximate calculation of the medial section based on a rounded off numerical series (see page 92). A simple method is to fold a sheet of paper in half three times in succession, lengthwise and breadthways. This divides the paper into eight parts from which the 3:5 ratio can be marked off (see lower diagram on this page).

The fewer spots, lines or shapes there are in the picture, the more precisely can their position within the picture area be determined. Consequently, the medial section can be applied with greatest success with simpler forms of composition.

The horizontal bridge (page 91) is divided by the man on the medial section. The ratio of black area to white is not in accordance with the medial section, but is in the ratio of about 1:4. This prevents the picture from being too well balanced and therefore monotonous.

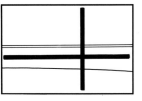

Medial section

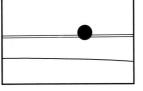

Dominating spot 26

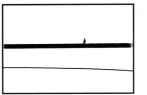

Horizontals 46

Verticals 48

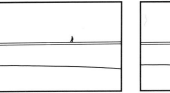

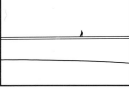

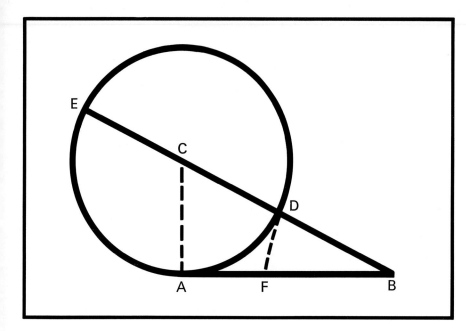

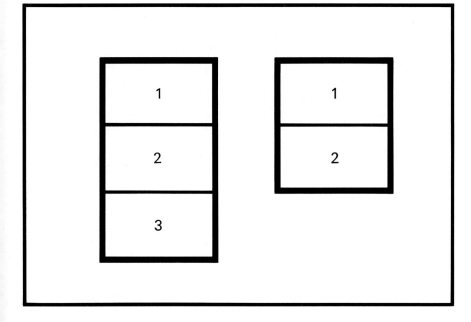

The upper diagram shows the precise geometrical construction for the medial section. But for the purposes of composition such accuracy is unnecessary. It suffices to work to the rounded off series of ratios (2:3, 3:5, 5:8, 8:13 etc.). These ratios are used in composition as, for instance by contrasting a group of three figures against one of five. Similarly, they can be applied to areas within a picture. These proportions are often found in architecture, above all in the relationship of the dimensions of doors and windows, as illustrated by the lower diagram on this page and the photograph on page 93. The medial section is not a thing to be applied too rigorously; it should be adapted to the photographer's own sense of balance.

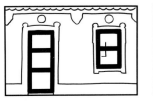

Medial section

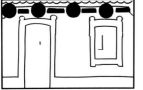

Visual line 34

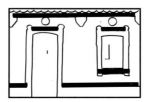

Horizontals 46

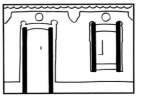

Verticals 50

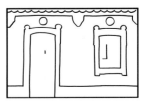

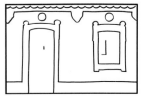

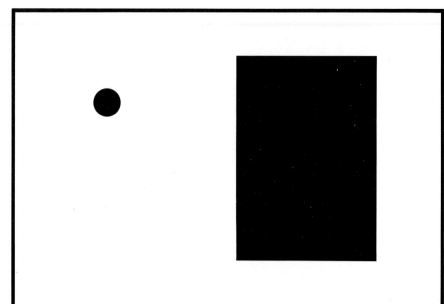

Size contrast
(large to small)

Verticals 50

Contrasting shapes 8.;

In extreme contrast to the balance of the medial section, widely differing sizes and quantities can be used as a basis for the composition—small shapes against large areas, large areas of darkness against small bright detail and vice versa. In the photograph above the delicate detail of the bird cages is strikingly contrasted with the large area of the doorway. Even when the subject comprises a number of similar features a contrast in quantities is possible—one man, for instance, sitting alone near a group of his companions (page 95).

In this case besides the pure contrast of numbers there is also that of group and individual. To what extremes this contrast in size relationships is taken is a matter for the taste of the individual photographer. The ultimate limit, however, is reached when the small element is so diminished in size that it has become merely a disturbing spot.

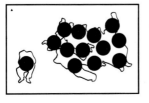
One against many

Distrubing spot 30

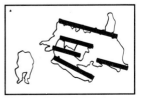
Verticals 50

Oblique lines 56

Visual shapes 66

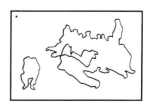

The position of the horizon can be used to emphasize the character of a landscape. There are no fixed rules; the horizon must be adapted in each case to the subject and the effect desired.

A low horizon, as on page 97, has a balanced effect and gives a strong visual impression of expansiveness. A high horizon, (upper picture, this page) gives an impression of heaviness. Here the landscape can be seen in some detail.

By omitting the horizon altogether, as in the lower picture on this page, the eye becomes free to concentrate entirely on detail. If, as here, there is a great deal of detail, the whole picture becomes a pattern. It is usually unsatisfactory to have the horizon passing through the middle of the picture as it divides the picture into two equal halves.

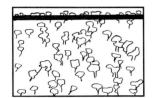

High horizon

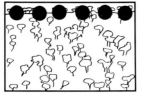

Visual line 34

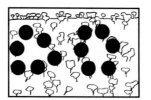

Visual shapes 40

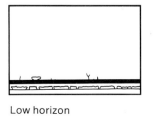

Low horizon

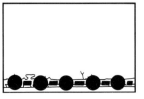

Visual line 34

Horizontals 46

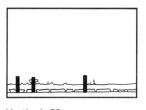

Verticals 50

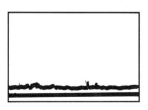

Contrasting lines 62

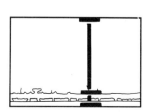

Contrasting areas 94

In general, the problems of spatial composition are the same in all branches of art. Nevertheless there are individual cases in which problems arise which are of little or no concern except to the photographer.

Whereas, for example, in cinematography the most important creative factor is movement, only in the exceptional case is that of importance to the still photographer. (See page 100).

In photography, certain technical difficulties arise which, however, if suitably dealt with can result in interesting pictures. Among these is depth of field. The photographic lens, and above all the longer focus lens, when set at any particular distance and stop can only render a limited range of distance as acceptably sharp. At close range this depth of field is very small. If this optical "defect" is deliberately exploited in pictorial composition, excellent pictures can be produced, especially in colour photography. On page 99 there is an example of unsharp foreground; the leaves close to the lens are out of focus. The two pictures on the left illustrate the different effects which can result from shifting the depth-of-field to different parts of a subject.

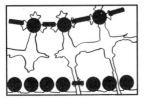

Visual lines 34

Horizontals 46

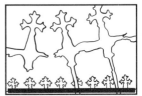

Oblique lines 56

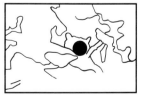

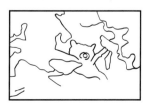

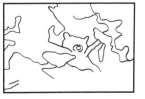

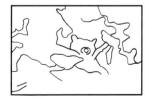

Dominating spot 26   Oblique lines 56

Blur due to movement

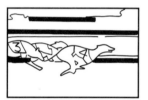
Horizontals 46

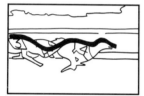
Wavy line 58

Triangle 70

Besides the use of depth of field as a medium of expression there is also blur due to subject movement, and background blur which results from "panning" the camera. Subject movement blur (with the camera stationary) occurs when the exposure is relatively long and the subject, or part of the subject, moves during the exposure (see photograph on page 43).

Background blur is familiar from such subjects as motor racing, where even at relatively fast shutter speeds, the rapid movement of the camera following the subject reduces the background to a mere streak. The subject itself remains sharp.

This effect does not have to be confined to fast moving subjects. Interesting results are possible with slow movement also.

In this case however, longer exposures are needed, otherwise the background movement does not show up sufficiently. The two examples were taken at $^1/_8$ and $^1/_{15}$ sec, and each was selected from a whole series of exposures. With panned exposures it is difficult to control the composition of the picture and the light and shade distribution. As with slow shutter speeds, there is the additional danger of camera shake, it is always necessary to make a series of exposures to be sure of a good result.

Dominating spot 26

Visual shape 40

Oblique lines 56

Verticals 50

Oblique lines 56

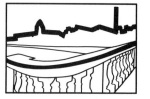
Contrasting lines 62

The use of extremely short focal length lenses as a medium of pictorial composition in photography and cinematography is a facility which we owe to technological development. Wide angle lenses have three main characteristics— great depth of field, over-emphasis of the foreground (see also page 14, optical illusion) and the distortion of verticals (converging verticals) even with only very slight camera tilt. Even at full aperture, depending upon the quality of the lens, everything in the field of view from 6–9 feet to infinity is in sharp focus. When a wide angle lens is stopped down, its depth of field is practically unlimited.

Converging verticals, objectionable as they normally are, when used deliberately can result in interesting pictures. For example, it is the slight distortion of the church on page 103 that gives it its surrealist character, while the over-emphasis of the bridge balustrade, above, enhanced the impression created by the buildings along the river bank.

Dominating spot 26

Verticals 50

Oblique lines 56

Triangle 70

Horizontals 46

Verticals 50

Triangles 70

Telephoto lenses, especially those of longer focus, such as 135 or 250 mm, have directly opposite characteristics to those of the wide angle lens. They have a very limited field of view and very shallow depth of field. A telephoto lens produces a compression of image planes and so automatically brings a kind of order into the picture.

In view of this it is perhaps not to be wondered at that more than half the illustrations in this book were taken with telephoto lenses.

In the close-up range, which, depending upon the construction of the particular lens, extends to a format-filling portrait, the wide angle lens by virtue of its very small depth of field at full, or nearly full aperture gives ideal separation between subject and background.

Naturally, telephoto lenses also help to bridge considerable distances, so that inaccessible subjects can be photographed at a scale which would otherwise be impossible. Thus, it was possible to photograph the facades above with a 250 mm lens from across a broad river. The fascination of the photograph on page 105 is due to the foreshortening of the row of columns. This compression of verticals permits the eye to travel into the depth of the picture, only rather slowly.

Dominating spot 26

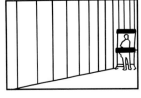

Horizontals 46

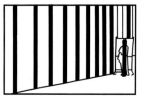

Verticals 50

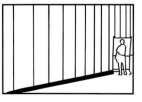

Oblique lines 56

Technical Data

Cameras:
Zeiss Ikon Contarex Special,
Contarex Professional and
Contarex Super with inter-
changeable magazine back

Lenses:
Carl Zeiss Distagon f/2.8,
  25 mm
Carl Zeiss Distagon f/2,
  35 mm
Carl Zeiss Planar f/2, 50 mm
Carl Zeiss Sonnar f/2, 85 mm
Carl Zeiss Sonnar f/4,
  135 mm
Carl Zeiss Sonnar f/4,
  250 mm
(Carl Zeiss,
Western Germany)
 Film:
 Adox KB 17 (40 ASA)
 Agfa ISS (125 ASA) and
 Kodak Tri-X (400 ASA).
 Developed in Rodinal, en-
  larged on Agfa Brovira
  developed in Eukobrom.

Countries of origin:
Germany (G), France (F),
Ireland (IRL), Italy (I),
Austria (A), East Africa (EA)
and Portugal (P).

11 The roofs of Nazare (P)
   250 mm, $^1/_{250}$ sec., f/8
13 Field path (P)
   135 mm, $^1/_{250}$ sec., f/5·6
14 Planes (F),
   35 mm, $^1/_{125}$ sec., f/8
15 Mafra Monastery (P),
   25 mm, $^1/_{60}$ sec., f/11
16 Lisbon, old town (P),
   50 mm, $^1/_{250}$ sec., f/5·6
17 Lake Manyara (EA),
   35 mm, $^1/_{30}$ sec., f/2
19 Empty bottles
   50 mm, $^1/_{125}$ sec., f/2·8

21 Massai herdsman (EA),
   85 mm, $^1/_{250}$ sec., f/8
22 Stone-pines (F),
   135 mm, $^1/_{125}$ sec., f/5·6,
   red filter
23 Student in the park
   (IRL),
   85 mm, $^1/_{250}$ sec., f/5·6
24 Façade (P),
   135 mm, $^1/_{250}$ sec., f/5·6
25 A rest in the park (G),
   50 mm, $^1/_{125}$ sec., f34
26 Façade (F),
   50 mm, $^1/_{250}$ sec., f/8
27 Cat (P),
   50 mm, $^1/_{60}$ sec., f/4
28 Boats (P),
   135 mm, $^1/_{250}$ sec., f/5·6
28 Suckling pigs (G),
   85 mm, $^1/_{125}$ sec., f/4
29 Boat (P),
   135 mm, $^1/_{250}$ sec., f/5·6
30 Little Portuguese girl (P),
   50 mm, $^1/_{60}$ sec., f/2·8–4
31 Boat and seagulls (IRL),
   50 mm, $^1/_{30}$ sec., f/2·8
32 Two windows (G),
   85 mm, $^1/_{250}$ sec., f/4
33 Two Irishmen (IRL),
   85 mm, $^1/_{250}$ sec., f/4
34 Lamps (Cairo),
   35 mm, $^1/_{30}$ sec., f/2·8
35 Jockeys (IRL),
   135 mm, $^1/_{250}$ sec., f/5·6
37 Cows on the beach (IRL),
   135 mm, $^1/_{250}$ sec., f/8
39 Shepherd and herd (P),
   135 mm, $^1/_{250}$ sec., f/5·6
40 Beach scene (P),
   25 mm, $^1/_{250}$ sec., f/8
41 Fish auction (P),
   85 mm, $^1/_{250}$ sec., f/8
43 Crossroads (G),
   35 mm, $1^1/_2$ min., f/5·6
45 Cartwheel (F),
   50 mm, $^1/_{250}$ sec., f/8–11
46 Flight of steps (P),
   85 mm, $^1/_{125}$ sec., f/11

47 Rocky shore (IRL),
135 mm, $1/250$ sec., f/5·6

49 Island (IRL),
125 mm, $1/250$ sec., f/5·6

50 Bookmaker (IRL),
85 mm, $1/60$ sec., f/2

51 Palms (EA),
135 mm, $1/250$ sec., f/11

52 Nazare (P),
85 mm, $1/250$ sec., f/5·6

53 Nazare (P),
50 mm, $1/250$ sec., f/8

54 On the beach (P),
50 mm, $1/250$ sec., f/8

55 Before the storm (P),
135 mm, $1/250$ sec., f/8

56 Landscape (IRL),
135 mm, $1/125$ sec., f/5·6

57 Cranes (G),
135 mm, $1/125$ sec., f/5·6–8

58 Park in Lisbon (P),
135 mm, $1/250$ sec,. f/8–11

59 Field path (A),
135 mm, $1/125$ sec., f/5·6

60 Dead tree (EA),
35 mm, $1/60$ sec., f/16

61 Rock crevices (IRL),
25 mm, $1/125$ sec., f/11

62 Contrast in lines (I),
50 mm, $1/125$ sec., f/8

63 Yachts in harbour (I),
135 mm, $1/125$ sec., f/5·6

64 Poles (G),
85 mm, $1/250$ sec., f/8

65 Ladder-beam (G),
50 mm, $1/60$ sec., f/4

66 Flamingoes (G),
135 mm, $1/125$ sec., f/4

67 Jumping Massai (EA),
85 mm, $1/250$ sec., f/8

68 Horsemen (IRL),
85 mm, $1/250$ sec., f/5·6

69 Irish village street (IRL),
135 mm, $1/125$ sec., f/5·6

70 Five women (P),
85 mm, $1/30$ sec., f/2

71 Gabels (IRL),
85 mm, $1/250$ sec., f/5·6–8

72 Doorway (IRL),
50 mm, $1/125$ sec., f/4

73 Triffic mirrors (P),
135 mm, $1/250$ sec., f/5·6

74 Cat in window (IRL),
50 mm,   sec., f/2·8

75 Row of windows (G),
85 mm, $1/250$ sec., f/8

76 Dog and grating (P),
50 mm, $1/250$ sec., f/8

77 Window (P),
50 mm, $1/60$ sec., f/2·8

78 Bark of plane tree (G),
50 mm, $1/60$ sec., f/4

79 Seascape (IRL),
135 mm, $1/125$ sec., f/8

80 Market-woman (P),
85 mm, $1/60$ sec., f/4

81 House painting (P),
135 mm, $1/250$ sec., f/8

82 Cottage (IRL),
250 mm, $1/125$ sec., f/5·6

83 Bookmakers' stands
(IRL),
135 mm, $1/250$ sec., f/8

85 Cart (P),
50 mm, $1/250$ sec., f/8

86 Girl and cat (P),
85 mm, $1/250$ sec., f/4

87 Landscape (A),
135 mm, $1/250$ sec., f/8

88 Bird (EA),
135 mm, $1/250$ sec., f/4

88 Stone blocks (IRL),
50 mm, $1/250$ sec., f/4

89 Field church (A),
135 mm, $1/125$ sec., f/5·6

91 New bridge (G),
135 mm, $1/250$ sec., f/11

93 Door and window (P),
35 mm, $1/250$ sec., f/5·6

94 In the doorway (P),
5 mm, $1/60$ sec.,   f/2·8
59 mm, $1/60$ sec., f/2·8

95 Fishermen on the beach (P),
35 mm, $1/250$ sec., f/8

96 Olive grove (P),
135 mm, $1/250$ sec., f/5·6

97 Herd of goats (EA),
    135 mm, $^1/_{250}$ sec., f/5·6
98 Railings (IRL),
    85 mm, $^1/_{250}$ sec., f/2·8
99 Raccoon (G),
    135 mm, $^1/_{125}$ sec., f/4
100 Greyhounds (IRL),
    50 mm, $^1/_8$ sec., f/4
101 Horseman (G),
    50 mm, $^1/_{15}$ sec., f/5·6
102 Dublin (IRL),
    25 mm, $^1/_{250}$ sec., f/11
103 Village church (P),
    25 mm, $^1/_{250}$ sec., f/8
104 Porto (P),
    250 mm, $^1/_{250}$ sec., f/5·6
105 Colonnade (P),
    250 mm, $^1/_{125}$ sec., f/11

Acknowledgements

Achim Dengle,
Page 66 (Flamingoes)
Page 101 (Horseman)

Karin Mante,
Page 62 (Contrast in lines)

Joachim Sändig,
Page 57 (Cranes)
Page 64 (Poles)

Wolfgang Stolte,
Page 105 (Colonnade).

All the remaining photos by
the author.